LEADFLUENCE

Secrets to Leading Others Inside Out
So They Can Achieve A Higher State Of
Performance

ROXANE BOBB-SEMPLE R.N.

DEDICATION

Dedicated to God for directing my path and for showing me that I cannot lean on my own understanding, and that he will never lead me wrong. I love you Lord.

To Mark, my husband, my partner, my soulmate, my everything. Thank you for your support, patience and belief in me. I love you.

To my parents, Merle and Sunday Akinmusire, my brothers, my nieces and nephews and my amazing friends. Shout outs to Michelle, Melissa and Amy, and my three beautiful angels in heaven for surrounding me with the beauty of faith, love and friendship. I am forever grateful. I love you all.

CONTENTS

TURNING POINT

"Do nothing from selfishness or empty conceit,
but with humility of mind regard one another as
more important than yourselves…" Philippians 2:3

Stagnation, lack of motivation and lack of engagement. Three years ago this was me. I spent ten years feeling like I was stuck in a cocoon with a beautiful butterfly inside, who was not given the opportunity to spread her wings and fly. My obstacle was that the climate was not right. I was a caterpillar with a big appetite for an extremely long time, just crawling on the ground, picking up whatever I could to add segments to myself. Eventually, I was stuck in the cocoon and became a caterpillar who stopped eating, stopped moving and stopped growing. I felt lifeless in my job. I did not see the opportunities for growth or at least the type of growth that I felt that I needed, and to be honest, I did not even know what that growth looked like. What I felt was, I did not have a degree or masters, so my experience and what I had to offer was not appreciated or recognized. In my heart, I knew that I was supposed to be doing something different, but did not know what.

Somehow, I came across a list of Canada's Top 100 Employers. The organizations were evaluated on the physical workplace, work atmosphere and social, health, financial and family benefits, vacation and time off, employee communications, performance management, training and skills development, and community involvement.

I realized that this award placed complete emphasis on the employees from a holistic perspective. The "goal is to attract and keep the best people and help them develop to their full potential," says Dr. Barry McAllen, President, and CEO of Sunnybrook Hospital one of Canada's Top 100 Employers for 2016.

In 2013, I decided to stretch out and grow my legs, grow my wings and open my eyes. During this process, I went through a lot of internal conflicts. I came to the shocking realization that I had fallen into a few traps. I thought that doing great work would get me recognized. I thought that my boss would market me because of my great work. I believed that self-promotion was being boastful and wrong. I felt that I needed to have a "title" to be a leader. I was wrong. That was when I decided that I needed to be my top employer first, and needed to lead myself. I needed to make sure that I was cautious of the work and social atmosphere that I placed myself. I was responsible for my health, financial security, family benefits, vacation and time off. It was also important for me to learn how to communicate with myself, to listen to my inner voice, and be attentive of what I allowed to enter my hard drive otherwise known as my brain. I needed to evaluate what performance level was acceptable to me per my standards. And it was important that I could be of service to others in every way possible. I needed to be my walking billboard. I needed my exact place at the table. I needed to present to the world how I wanted to be perceived based on my values and not someone else's.

I decided to be the goldfish on the outside of the fish bowl and leave the bedside in the acute care facility to develop and grow to a higher state of performance and explore other leadership styles.

I then went to work for a corporation, on Canada's Top 100 Employers list, where my talents, skills, experience and everything I had to offer was important, rather than just considering which or how many degrees I could bring to the table. Being a walking billboard was not frowned upon, it was encouraged.

I flourished, my wings were spread wide. I saw opportunities for growth, impact and use of my skills and talents. I was referred to as a woman of influence, a leader and a woman of credibility. This was something new to me, and I was a bit confused, as I did not know what it meant and how it pertained to me.

As an acute care nurse these were words I never heard, they were words that I expected to be used to describe a manager, not an employee. Within this corporation, I shed many tears, and they were tears of joy, fulfillment and belonging. My talents and all that I had to offer were recognized. It had nothing to do with who I could rub noses with, but rather with my capabilities. I was presented with many opportunities that allowed me to grow as a leader. If I sought out opportunities, it was well received and encouraged. Although I was happy in the corporate world, I still wrestled with mixed emotions. In my quest to discover and experience better leadership, I had to leave behind what I truly loved, looking after patients physically. My discomfort lead me to dive even deeper into learning about personal and leader development and how to take myself to a higher state of performance so that I could live my best life. It pushed me to commit to sharing my knowledge and experience with other leaders, so that they can lead from the inside out and avoid losing their best employees due to poor leadership. This experience has taught me that many leaders struggle with aligning their essential self with who they are so they can connect, unite, transform and empower others and effectively "show up" to the world. Understanding the difference between power and positive influence will impact their leadership.

Armed with this experience, knowledge, and my extensive healthcare background, I set out to share the lessons I had learned, with a particular focus in healthcare but also knowing that this information would apply to most professions and individuals, whether they are students, parents, or entrepreneurs.

I have discovered that too many healthcare frontline managers are missing a significant skill - how to be a leader and how to develop leaders on a multi-dimensional level. The funny thing is that leadership is something that we already have within us, we just need to nurture and grow it. Poor leadership is the reason why many employees do not feel valued, respected or heard by their employers. Many frontline healthcare managers were once former bedside nurses who have been recognized for their exceptional contribution to the organization and were placed into a leadership position without having or being provided opportunities to gain the knowledge, experience, or education to be successful as a leader. Most importantly too many of them are placed in these positions without ever experiencing for themselves how real leadership works. Unfortunately, under these circumstances, they never become as clear as they should on what their personal leadership development brand is and how they can apply it to their newly acquired leadership role. And if they enter the position with a strong sense of their personal leadership development brand, it quickly gets swallowed up by their daily managerial tasks.

Many studies have demonstrated that 70% of leadership training comes from on the job training, but unfortunately too often, on the job training is provided by other frontline managers, who have not themselves developed their personal leadership brand and skills, leading to a ripple effect. Furthermore, leadership should not be about training people, but it should be about developing them to be leaders over time.

My mission has been to educate emerging, and seasoned leaders who have the heart for learning, serving and loving others. I help them position themselves so that they become intentional about their standard of leader development and skills. I assist them to build their confidence and capabilities to get clear on their leadership style so that they can lead others from a place of positive influence vs. power. In turn, this helps them attract and retain the best team members, and keep them engaged, happy and motivated. I am proud of the significant role I get to play in supporting individuals on this journey of owning their greatness and growing them to a higher state of performance so that they can make a difference in their lives and the lives of others.

With so much information available, my intent is to prevent leaders from becoming 'info-junkies.' Info junkies are the ones who have loads of information, tons of resources available and hundreds of plans to execute, yet still fail to make a mark. They do not take action, and their plans are mostly impractical.

You will learn a lot within these pages, and you will be able to put your learning to good use. But remember it is only on paper, they are only words, and only as good as what you do with them. So for best results, you will need to take action.

So who should be reading my book? The answer is everyone. I am not just saying this for the sake of saying it. You should know who you are, how you "show up" in the world and what you represent to the world. When you walk out of that room and people start to talk about you, what they say should align with what you would say about yourself.

Whether you are in the healthcare field or not, as long as you have the desire to make a difference in the world, if your dreams are so big that they seem impossible, if you are discontent with the status quo, or if you simply want to grow others, then I can guarantee you that you are indeed reading the right book. You will be able to take what you have learned in this book and apply it to your personal life, career, and business. And regardless of the nature of what you do, the result is the same. You will have learned to align your core essence with what you love doing, and nurture strong and lasting relationships through connection and unity, to transform yourself so you can empower others and become the ultimate leader of your tribe.

Leader development has become my passion, and I love sharing and teaching what I have learned. It is important to me to provide my insight from the perspective of the employee, the reason and benefits of improved leader development. As John Maxwell said, "everything rises and falls on leadership." Developing your leadership skills will not only make an impact in your workplace, but it will also make you a better person as a whole.

God Bless You,
Roxane Akinmusire - Bobb-Semple R.N

RECLAIM YOUR TRUE ESSENCE

"You are essentially who you create yourself to be and all that occurs in your life is the result of your own making." - Stephen Richards

It is essential to understand that the journey through leadership development starts with you. I am sure you have heard the saying "treat others the way you would want to be treated." Knowing how to lead yourself first before you can be a leader to anyone else is the first step in your development. Your mind, body and soul are the vehicle for creating the impact you want to make in the world. And, if they are not in the right place your mind, body and soul will not be used to their full potential and you will be doing yourself and the world a disservice. So it is important to nurture and align your physical, psychological, spiritual and day-to-day wellbeing from the inside out.

Leadership is not only about skills and actions, and it is not about how many degrees or letters you have behind your name. I know most people are proud of theirs - I know I am proud of mine - however the reality is that leadership is also about your presence and the energy that you give off which can positively impact those you lead.

When I started on my leader development journey, I had to peel back all the layers that I allowed to cover and enter my bubble. I felt so naked, but I knew I had to do it if I ever wanted to be the leader that I knew was hiding in me. I had to be mindful as to how my energy and my presence impacted those with whom I came into contact with. I had to come face to face with my own vulnerability because it was staring me straight in the face. Trust me this was not easy nor comfortable. It is still is a constant work in progress for me, but it has become better and easier over time.

I had to take a look at who I was as a whole and not as partial segments. Yes, I still work to develop and nurture each segment, but I continually make every effort to frequently check back to ensure they are in alignment with each other and make up the whole I intend to be.

Physically, I knew that I was not treating my body right. I would feed it all sorts of unhealthy food. I would get only three to four hours of sleep each night and being a shift worker did not help. I was tired all the time and rarely exercised.

"I was tired of being tired." It was so bad that I internalized the phrase "I am tired." It became the first thing that came out of my mouth when anyone would ask me how I was doing.

I made the decision to start eating right and to at least get eight hours of sleep every night and exercise regularly. In all honesty, to this day it is a challenge, but I have noticed the difference. I feel so much better that I have reduced the use of my most famous words " I am tired" by seventy-five percent!

When your body is being feed toxic food, and by toxic I mean processed and high sugar foods, and it is deprived of an opportunity to rejuvenate itself during sleep, you become cranky, your vibration is low, you anger easily, your patience is almost non-existent. It does not make you a person that anyone would want to follow if they had a choice. Neither would they want to be around you. It is time to reprogram your physical being.

I had to work on my mindset and envision what healthy to me looked like. I had to change what I use to say: "I am tired." I had to remind myself that no matter what I was doing 9:00PM was and is to this day my bedtime, and I had to ensure that others respected that. It meant not answering the phone, texts or emails and removing the TV from the bedroom. I also had to create balance for myself and not push myself beyond what I was capable of doing. I also decided to reconsider what I allowed to infuse my soul, which actually lead me to the redevelopment of my spiritual life. Since then my spiritual life has guided my steps.

It has showed me what I needed to be doing, where I needed to be, and what I should allow to enter my space. My physical, psychological and spiritual journey has lead me to reach clarity on my day-to-day well-being. I know what works for me to create my balance and focus, and I want the same for you.

Identifying the fundamental you is a step that cannot be missed, because if you do not work on it, and go through the process, there will always be a missing link to your leadership puzzle and over time your ship will sink. Many think this step is too much work, sometimes too painful so it is often bypassed. I would agree that yes it takes a lot of work, and yes it can be painful, but the rewards outweigh the pain. If you try to avoid this process, what ends up happening is that you have to come back to it at some point along the journey. Rediscovering your "essential you" through physical, psychological, spiritual and day to day well-being is the foundation, and it will keep the building from collapsing. If you skip this process, the building will not be able to sustain an earthquake. Your well-being is not just given to you. You have to take action and create it.

PHYSICAL WELL-BEING

With the heavy demands that society places upon us, it is important to seek programs and ways to enhance your physical well-being on your continuous journey through leader development. The activities that you engage in and the daily choices that you make affect the way you feel physically and eventually psychologically.

Nutrition

The first thing that you need to look at is your nutrition. What are you putting in your body to fuel it daily? Are these foods as close to their natural state as possible? How do you feel once you have digested your food? Being mindful of how food makes you feel is important. Does it make you foggy, sleepy, sluggish or give you a burst of energy and then a crash? If it does, then it is not good for your body. We have enough environmental toxins that we are exposed to on a daily bases, that we need to make a conscious decision not to put toxic foods in our bodies.

Take the time necessary to learn about nutrition, how it fuels your body and improves your energy levels and brain power.

Sleep

When we make sleep one of our priorities, mainly getting seven to eight hours of true restful sleep, we wake up feeling recharged and ready to take on the world in the morning.

There are three stages to the sleep cycle, from light sleep Stage 1 to Stage 3, which is a deeper sleep. Each stage lasts about ninety minutes and repeats itself. As you sleep you move through these stages, but you spend most of your time in the lighter stages, which are Stages 1 and 2.

Stage 1: you are drowsy, drifting in and out of sleep, but you can still hold a conversation. You toss and turn and eventually fall asleep, but can be easily disrupted, which often leaves you feeling like you did not sleep at all. Stage 2: is where we spend most of our sleep time, about fifty percent. In this stage you are asleep, but if you do hear a sound you would awaken and not be able to make sense of it. Stage 3: many people never reach this stage, it is the phase where you do not respond to the outside environment. You do not respond to sound or other stimuli. This stage is needed for your organs to detoxify, your kidneys to clean your blood, and your body to replace cells, heal wounds, and build muscle tissues. At the end of Stage 3, REM (Rapid Eye Movement) occurs and you dream. The good thing is that studies show we only need 20% of deep sleep each night, which works out to be 1.5 to 1.8 hours in eight to nine hours of sleep. Because it takes a while to get to the deep sleep phase, as adults, you need at least eight hours of sleep.

Exercise

Take at least 30 minutes a day to do some form of exercise. I know you have heard this before so I am not going to harp too much on it here. The main point is that it does not have to be vigorous, it can be as simple as a brisk walk. You will have heard at some point in your life about the benefits of exercise. The fact is that it really does help with circulating blood throughout the body, and allows fresh oxygen to enter your body to restore those cells that have been working tirelessly. It helps to clear up fogginess.

Strengthen Your Immune System

Your immune system is always fighting for you, because it knows if it does not, sickness will cause havoc in your body. We have to be nice to our immune system and not stress it out or make its job harder. Eat the right foods, get plenty of rest and enough exercise. It is important to keep your immune system strong. Having the right balance is the key as the immune system is not a separate entity; it needs to have everything in working order to function properly.

PSYCHOLOGICAL WELL-BEING

Happiness, contentment, enjoyment, self-confidence, engagement, self-esteem, and knowing that you can do the things you want to do, is all part of maintaining your psychological well-being. You have to choose what you focus on. You need to wake up every morning making a conscious decision to be happy, to be active, and to protect your time including making time for yourself. You need to have a sense of humor, see the funny side of things and boost your self-esteem with positive thoughts and sayings.

It is always an excellent idea to have someone with whom you can bounce off thoughts and ideas. Protecting your hard-drive, your mind is paramount. Be very mindful of what you allow to enter there. One thing I do is to stick post-it notes all over the house, especially in the bathroom and the kitchen with inspirational quotes, to keep my mind in the right frame.

SPIRITUAL WELL-BEING

Spiritual well-being ties nicely into psychological well-being. Your spiritual well-being involves discovering your values, beliefs and your purpose. We will discuss this further a little later in this book. Connecting with God and yourself will allow you to see life from a whole different perspective and understand what it truly means to be happy.

I take time during the mornings to be still and listen to what God is saying to me about my assignment for the day. I think of how lucky I am to have woken up to see another day and to be able to sit and walk upright so I can tackle the world and make an impact. I am grateful that I can also see the beauty of the world and hear its beautiful sounds. I thank God that I am not alone and I have a safe and warm place to rest my body at night. I make sure I thank God for everything, even for the things that are not so perfect in my life because it gives me an opportunity to learn, be better and course correct.

ACTION STEPS TO TAKE NOW

1. Start your day at 5AM.

2. Before you roll out of bed, take two minutes to show gratitude for at least two things/people. Say "I am grateful now that... or "thank you for...." (finish the sentence) - you can also stick post-it notes around the house.

3. Sit up at the side of your bed. Close your eyes and ask God to show you what you are supposed to do today and to show you whose life you are meant to touch today. Do not forget that today you choose to be happy.

4. Now stand up at your bedside and complete at least 30 minutes of physical activity.

5. Plan your meals for the day - make sure they are made of ingredients as close to their natural state as possible.

6. Set your alarm for 9PM, this is the time you should be going to bed to wake up for 5AM the following day.

.

REDISCOVER YOUR CORE BRAND VALUES

"Leadership is doing what is right even when no one is watching" - Anonymous

You are a leader. You have led at some point in life, whether at home, amongst friends, in the office or in the community.

As John Quincy Adams stated, "If your actions inspire others to dream more, learn more, do more and become more, you are a leader." You have a lot to offer to the world and your role as a leader must be taken seriously. It speaks to your strengths and talents and the value you offer to those you serve.

Your actions and decisions are always being watched and evaluated. People want to see if they have any connection with you. They want to understand how you came up with your decisions and why you did what you did. They also evaluate you to see if you are living up to the standard that you have publicly shared with them. Often there are incongruences in how the world sees your actions and decisions versus how you intended them to be perceived. Some of you may be great leader at work or in the business community, yet be less than stellar in your leadership role at home. And, some may be great leaders at home, yet fall short at work. The relevant question here is why? Why would the driving force for your actions and decisions be different at home than at work? I can guarantee you that it has to do with the fact that you need to understand what your core values are and whether you or someone else scripted them.

I was presented with the concept of core values a few years ago. I had no idea why I made certain decisions and what drove my actions on many occasions. I just made decisions because it just felt right at the time or someone was telling me that it was right. Now that I reflect back there were many occasions when there were inconsistencies.

Rediscovering and identifying my core values were fascinating. I now know how to formulate and articulate my personal values, so I can share them with others and be held accountable.

I never realized how many of my core values were the result of someone else saying that it was the way it had to be. Needless to say, I released a few of those values that were not aligned with what I believed. Today I have my core values up on my wall by the entrance of my home, so that I can be reminded of them each day and also for those who enter my home to see, so they know as well, and they can hold me accountable.

As a leader your personal core values are vital and you probably already know in your mind what they are, but for people looking from the outside in, do they see the same values in you? Your personal core values hold you accountable to walk the walk, so it most definitely needs to be shared with your team, and the people that surround you.

It is crucial to be aware of any shortfalls because your values are the attributes those who come into contact with you on a daily basis should be able to use to describe you. If these values do not align with who you are and what you represent, it is time to release them and create a new set of values and personal statement.

I want you to look in the mirror. What do you see? When someone sees your reflection, what do they see? What is your tribe saying about you when you walk out of the room? Is it in-line with what you would say about yourself if you left the room?

Take a moment and think of someone who you regard highly as a leader, and it does not have to be a celebrity because there are many more leaders directly in our lives than celebrities. How do they appear to you? If you compared notes with someone else would they be similar? What would you consider to be their personal statement?

To be clear and to ensure you understand the

messages I intend to share with you here, I am going to use celebrity leaders as examples. If we compared notes on Mother Theresa, Princess Diana, Oprah Winfrey and Richard Branson, I am sure the values that we would each come up with to describe them would be similar. I am also sure that they would be similar to the values they have for themselves. These individuals have been consistent in expressing themselves on a daily basis to the public about what is important to them and what they stand for.

It is time for you to communicate who you truly are or people will do it for you, and the results may not be aligned with your intentions .

ACTION STEPS TO TAKE NOW

I want you to work through the following questions with complete honesty.

Exercise #1:

What results do you want to achieve in the next year? Take some time to actually write it down. I have provided some space so you can jot your thoughts down. (this may change throughout the year or your lifetime)

My example:

To develop inspired and driven leaders to reach

their full potential and enhance their confidence, so that they can step into their leadership boots to empower and create other leaders.

_____

_____

_____

_____

Exercise #2:

What is important to you and what is unique about you? Write down every idea that comes to your mind in response to this question, there is no right or wrong answers. Try to write down at least 20 to 25 ideas.

My example:

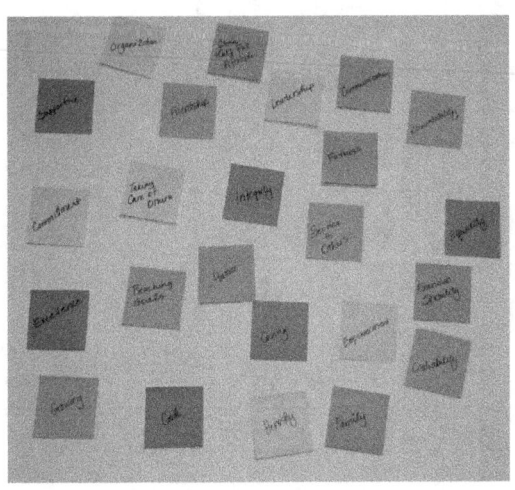

Exercise #3:

Now gather all of the words you wrote down into common groups of similar meaning or theme. For example "fairness" and "honesty" may be grouped together. Try to create 6 groups.

My example:

_____

_____

_____

Exercise #4:

Within the six groups look for a word that will summarize the entire group. This word will become one of your six personal core values.

My example:

Integrity, commitment, empowerment, service, excellence, accountability

_____

_____

Exercise #5:

Now write out a statement using these core values. The sentence starts like this, "I want to be known for ….." These core values are values that you have whether at home or in public spaces. They are what you live by and generally do not change much.

My example:

I want to be known for my integrity, commitment, empowerment, service, excellence and accountability.

_____

_____

_____

_____

Exercise #6:

Now combine these six words in two to three word phrases that reflect your desired identity.

My example:

commitment to excellence, empowering through service, integrity maintains accountability.

_____

_____

_____

_____

Exercise #7

Let's combine, exercise #1 and exercise #6 to formulate your personal core values statement.

My example:

I am known for being committed to excellence, empowering others through service and having integrity to be accountable. This allows me to develop inspired and driven leaders to reach their full potential and enhance their confidence, so that they can step into their leadership boots to empower and create other leaders.

_____

_____

_____

_____

_____

Congratulations! You have just created your personal core values statement, otherwise known as your vision and mission statement. So, the big question is can you live up to your statement now that you have created it? Is this truly who you are? Your personal statement will evolve overtime, and for sure it may be challenging at first, however, if you place your statement where you can see it daily, as a constant reminder, living by it should not be that hard. Look at or think of your personal statement before you react or make any decision.

This will ensure that you can stay in alignment with your definition of you.

RECONNECT WITH YOUR PURPOSE

"The two most important days in your life are the day you are born and the day you find out why" -
Mark Twain

Before we get into the nitty-gritty of leadership, there is something that is imperative to get clear first. Why on earth are you going on this leader development journey? Why have you been called or chosen to be a leader?

Understanding why, and your purpose here on earth is critical and very simple. It is to be of service to others, without forgetting who you truly are. Service will present itself in a different format or on a different platform for everyone; whether it is through being a parent, brother, sister, friend, professional or entrepreneur. We need to inspire each other, empower and help every person that we come in contact with by sharing our skills, talents, knowledge and experience. If you have this mentality and live by it, your work here is done, and you will have great fulfillment. I have studied great leaders in the world and the one that inspired me the most was Steve Jobs, founder and CEO, of Apple Inc. His purpose and his mission were to "make a contribution to the world, by making tools for the mind that advanced humankind." It was not about the product or service, rather it was about how he could create a product that would improve everyone's quality of life. His *why* was very clear to the public, and this is why his company was so successful.

This lead to every tech company aspiring to be like Apple. However, the difference was that many of these tech companies were only out to make seemingly better products on the surface, without having the consumers' needs and well-being in mind to create a fantastic core product.

One of my favorite analogies by branding expert, Karen Kang of Branding Pays, states that when we look at a cake, the first thing that we see is the icing and the beautiful design on it. This is no doubt the first thing that attracted us to that particular cake and peaked our curiosity about its taste. If we like its look, we automatically think that the cake will taste great. Unfortunately that is not always the case.

Now, compare yourself to the cake. Your outer appearance, talents, knowledge, and degrees are the icing on the cake.

To be a leader what matters is the actual taste of the cake. This is what makes the cake, a good cake. The cake is the core of who you are, and this is what you have to work on before you can lead anyone else. The taste, consistency, appearance, and texture of the cake need to be the same throughout. My goal in this section is to help you get your cake right by helping you build the foundation to reclaim and connect with your purpose.

When I was working as a nurse in the acute care setting, my main focus was designing the icing on the cake with certificates after certificates and dabbling into different areas of nursing to make the design on the outside of my cake look good. I lost sight of my purpose and *why* I was doing all of that in the first place. I came to the point when I was just doing it to keep busy rather than face the reality that I was unhappy with where I saw my career going, and the fact that I would be stuck doing the same thing until I retired. I was afraid to start over and leave what I had known for so many years. Until finally one day, enough was enough. I needed to get out of that space to get clarity, to make space for amazing things to come into my life. My assignment is to be a leader, and I believe it is yours as well. It will look different for many of us. However, it will lead to similar results like positively impacting others' lives and helping them be the best they can be, and seeing others as equals, regardless of social and educational status.

Steve Jobs built Apple's brand to the point that many aspired to copy his model, yet none of the tech companies were fully able to master it. Apple was concerned about the whole cake while the other companies were only concerned with developing the icing on the cake, and not the cake itself.

When leading your team, you need to understand the people within your team and what motivates them as well as what motivates your decisions and actions, on a daily bases, which you explored in the previous chapter.

At the start of your career, your goal and most logical next steps are to work your way up the ladder, for better pay, more prestige, more perks, more control, etc. While being in a leadership position may have all these benefits, there is a bigger benefit to your role. The reality is that this role is not an easy one. This position requires you to be transparent, authentic, and mindful. To do this, you have to be clear on your *why* and why you have been called to do this.

If you are not crystal clear right now, let's get it straight right away.

Imagine a parent who has a child who presents many behavioral issues. The parent can easily give up, or they can re-evaluate why they chose to have children in the first place and why getting the child back on the right path is important to them. I can almost guarantee, that the parent will try to get the child on the right track. The parent's *why* is because their child is a representation of their parenting, as well as they, want something bigger and better for the child they love. So by identifying their *why*, the parents will pull out every source of energy from their well to try and help their child and improve the situation. This kind of mentality is similar to what leaders who lead a team should have. It is about digging deep and looking beyond all the noise and identifying your real purpose and *why* you were chosen to lead your tribe, so that when the earthquake hits, you will quickly dismiss your first instinct to run.

ACTION STEPS TO TAKE NOW

Being in a leadership role is a huge responsibility, and often it is not an easy task, so to help build your leader development foundation, I want you to think hard, dive deep and answer the following questions as to why you are or want to be a leader.

Why do you want this or why do you think you were called to be a leader?

_____

_____

_____

_____

What is it that attracted you to this leadership position?

_____

_____

_____

_____

Is it because you see it as a way to touch peoples' lives and be of service to them?   _____

Is it because you want to help those you lead grow and reach their own goals and dreams?

_____

Is it because you want to positively and intentionally influence those you lead to accomplish a common goal and vision? _____

If you answered "yes" to the last 3 questions, you are well on your way to achieving great things in your leadership role. If you answered "no", that is okay too, that's exactly why you picked up this book in the first place, so do not worry. I will help you understand what leadership truly is, and help you become the best leader you can be, so you can walk in your leadership boots.

REPOSITION YOUR SPOTLIGHT

"He must increase, I must decrease" John 3:30

Now let us get into the nitty-gritty of leadership. Great leaders are always focused on change, transformation, inclusion, and development. Leadership is more than just success. It is about making a significant impact on your tribe, through personal growth, reflection and learning how you can motivate your tribe to come on the journey with you to make things happen, now that you have identified your *why*.

Moving forward in life, career or business will come with challenges, and there is always the fear of failure. Sometimes, it may feel like the higher you climb, the more lonely it feels, but it does not have to be that way, as long as you have developed authentic relationships with others and helped them grow.

Moving your employees beyond the need for survival, where they feel that their job is much more than about the money, to a place where their job excites them and that they feel they are valuable to their employer is the first step to avoid losing your building blocks also known as your team.

Leadership is a process and will take some work to develop. It is learning to lead with focus, clarity, creativity and compassion so that those you influence can help you make things happen and make a positive difference within your organization. It is about you being in the background, storing away your pride and arrogance and seeing your employees for who they could be and not who they are at the moment. Help them develop and meet their personal development goals.

As humans, we all have a need for security, and there are some insecurities and feelings of being easily threatened when you see your employees climb. It may worry you, so you undermine them, whether consciously or unconsciously, as you try to guard your position. You try to put yourself clearly above and ahead. Those you lead will recognize this mindset. Your employees will begin to look for another hill to climb, and unfortunately these will likely end up being your best employees. Keep in mind employees do not want to leave the people that they work with, they leave the job when the work environment is poor.

When people feel they have to follow you because they have no other choice, that is a weak environment. It becomes a developed mentality that they are only at their job to meet their first and basic need, getting a paycheque so that they can have food and shelter. In this case, it is not because they want to follow you. You will get from them the minimal requirements necessary to get the job done, little energy, little motivation and you will have them watching their watches every minute of their working hours.

Just like in the earlier example of the parent with the child in trouble, your employees are a reflection of you and how well you lead them, and not about your management skills in handling the budget, resources, staffing, solving problems, implementing rules and regulations or the usual day to day things. It is much bigger than that. Your role goes beyond the position, because "the position" never actually has a safety net. Jobs come and go. When you are of service to others and create other leaders within the organization that is what makes the position worth having, and that is your safety net.

Remember, you have accomplished great things already that is why this position was offered to you. You must use it wisely, and help and grow those that you lead. Position them for success, as they are a reflection of your leadership, and imagine how it will feel to have developed other leaders. Real leaders are not in the spotlight, they reposition the spotlight so that the fruit of their labor is.

ACTION STEPS TO TAKE NOW

- During your next one on one with your employees ask them what they would like to accomplish personally in the next five years - and it has to be non-professional.

- Also ask them how you can help them accomplish one of their professional goals.

REACTIVATE YOUR TEAM RELATIONSHIPS

"Everyone can be great...because anyone can serve." - Dr. Martin Luther King

Now that you have completed some self-reflection and developed a relationship with yourself, you need to develop relationships with your employees. Connect with them, do not wait until they connect with you because it can be intimidating for them. Walk down the ladder to meet them. Talk with them, find out what they like doing and what their goals are personally and professionally. Find out how they perceive you, as their leader, how they feel about you and how you can help them accomplish their goals. Find out at least three non-professional facts about your employees when you have an opportunity to speak with them. Be present. Your employees want to know that you care for and about them? How can you assist them? Can they trust you? Do you have their best interest at heart and in mind or are you just manipulating them? You need to be a good listener so that you can help them get what they want or need. Have an open door policy. Your employees should not feel like your office is a space of negativity. Leave the door open.

Just remember, all employees can be managed the same, but not all employees can be lead the same.

Each employee has a different temperament, different passion, different dreams and goals and different motivating factors. Observe your employees' behaviors, this will tell you so much about them. Observing them will help you guide them in the right direction to grow. Employees are dying to give their leaders permission to lead them, so how can you make it easier for them? Your employees work with you, not for you. Work together as a team and create positive results. Employees are the most valuable assets of any organization, regardless of the type of organization you are in. Without these employees, your organization would not be able to function. Without happy employees, you will not have client satisfaction and the "wow factor" necessary to prosper your business.

You may be thinking that by building a relationship with your employees that you may not be respected, will appear to be soft, and will be taken advantage of. You would be wrong. As a leader your initial interactions are not there to build friendships, however you are there to create positive relationships. Building a positive relationship with your employees is the way that you behave and deal with each other, according to the Merriam-Webster Dictionary. Sit down with your team and have them come up with the house rules and the core values of the team. This now puts the responsibility on to the them to walk the walk instead of them being told they have to walk the walk. It makes work more enjoyable for all involved. Therefore, it increases retention, the energy level, motivation, and opens the channels of communication by fostering trust and adding value to each other. These are the results you obtain when team members feel that they have an impact and that they have contributed to shaping the team.

Yes, it is human nature for some to take your kindness for weakness. And, because you empower them, they may think it means that they can do anything they want. You may need to have one-on-ones with those individuals and remind them the team's goals, vision, and core values so that everyone is on the same page. Their reaction may be a symptom of a crack in the overall communication.

You will be tempted to ignore these individuals because it is "too complicated" to deal with them, but don't. Be transparent. Speak with those individuals as they may have personal issues that they are dealing with or they may have different values that do not align with those chosen by the team, which may force the individual to rethink if that environment is right for them. At least by speaking with them you, as well as the individual, will get clarity, and the issue can be resolved.

Keep sight of the primary goal to help others, work together, move forward and achieve. You need to find the right balance, which will be a trial and error process. Ensure your employees feel like stakeholders, that they do have an impact on the team, and that they are not just an employee number.

As a leader, listen more than you speak, so that you can understand. You may not have the answer, and that is okay. As a leader you do not need to know everything because truthfully no one does. You just need to know how to direct your team to find the answer. There might be someone on your team whose strength is research, delegate the task to them to find the answer and present it back to the team. As employees, we love this because it gives us a chance to ensure our voice is heard. You need to be in the continual mindset of being service minded. Your constant question should be "How can I help them?"

ACTION STEPS TO TAKE NOW

- Set up a team meeting to come up with the team core values and mission.

- Have the team's core values and mission printed and framed. Place it in a location where the team will see it on a daily basis.

.

REBUILD BY EMPOWERING OTHERS

"The beauty of empowering others is that your own power is not diminished in the process." - Barbara Colours

Working together with your employees to get things done allows you to gain influence, credibility, momentum, and increase morale, as well as to decrease turnover and reach achievable goals. Everyone becomes productive on all levels. And, it allows you to take your employees to another level of effectiveness while you create an environment of success within your team, department or company, which in turns draws other highly effective and productive people.

Many organizations do not go any further once they have met the first two needs of people, which based on Maslow's Hierarchy five needs theory are money and job security. While the organization has meet these needs, as a leader you need to meet your employees third need of belonging and feeling loved. Once you have built authentic relationships with your employees, working with them becomes easy. They will partner with you to get things done. Employees become more effective if they feel respected, that their opinion matters and that they are challenged with new tasks or increased responsibilities.

They need to feel like they can have an opportunity to shine, and get their work and talents recognized. Often, during presentations at large conferences or directly to other organizations, very rarely do you find that there is any front line staff involved in the process or the presentation. Very rarely do front line staff even know what the presentation is all about or even involved in gathering the data or the information needed to prepare the presentation. This type of approach does not show employees that they are a valued addition to their department.

If you think that your employees do not want to be involved, you're wrong! They do. Some may need a little encouragement and a manager/leader to tell them "you know what, I see that you have this particular talent, and I think that you have a lot to offer and you would be a great addition to the team." I can guarantee you that if you use this type of language, that you will get the biggest smile from that employee, or maybe even tears because this may be the first time they hear anything like it.

I encourage you to come up with a rewards and recognition program. Find ways to increase team engagement. Everyone has ideas on how they can make things better; give them the opportunity to share them. Encourage employees to come up with ideas that they feel would benefit the team and organization. If employees' ideas are implemented within your team or broader organization, provide them with a small token of appreciation to say "thank you...great job."

How about a monthly "I appreciate you" program? This will increase staff morale as well. It can be departmental or organization-wide. On a monthly basis, staff can send appreciation notes to other staff members they want to thank for something that they did. At the end of the month put all the names of those who received an appreciation, in a draw and pick a name. Award the individual with a small token of appreciation that was chosen by the sender, like a coffee-shop gift card, flowers, a few authorized hours off, a mention in a newsletter - anything goes so you can get creative.

What about throughout the year. Frontline staff members are nominated for something they did that was outstanding and recognizable. At the end of the year, their names are put forward for the big win, where they are awarded something from their bucket list or given cash valued gift card that they can use towards their bucket list item.

In healthcare, the budget is always a concern, and there never seems to be enough money to go around, again get creative. Awards do not always have to be around education success, which is common in the healthcare industry. Healthcare workers do not get enough recognition for the great job that they do, and it is time that they start to get recognized.

In healthcare, having a mobile massage company come every day or a few times a week to provide 10 mins massages, would show that you understand your employees' aches and pains with sore backs, shoulders, knees and feet. This gesture will rejuvenate them to come back out on the floor and give their best work, and also help you be the compassionate leader you aspire to be.

Rewards and recognition have become imperative in the workplace, particularly for the millennials, otherwise known as Generation Y (people born between 1980's and early 2000's), whom, studies show, have a decreased attention span. It takes a lot more to impress and keep them in one spot, than it did with their predecessors. Millennials are constantly looking for growth and what is in it for them. Rewards and recognitions are an important means to keep them engaged. Growing others become imperative when you are leading this group.

ACTION STEPS TO TAKE NOW

- Brainstorm with your team to come up with ideas for a rewards and recognition program and speak to the appropriate person to get it implemented.

RELEASE OTHER LEADERS

"Leaders don't create followers they create more leaders." - Tom Peters

As a leader, the question is not how you are doing but rather how are the people you are leading doing? Are they growing and being promoted? If you are ever unsure of how you are doing as a leader, take a look at those you lead, and you will get your answer.

Remember when I mentioned earlier that your team is a reflection of you? They truly are. Real leaders create more leaders, not followers. Equip them and release them. Provide them with the tools and mindset necessary to be successful in whichever direction they go, and they hopefully will return the favor to those that they lead.

Your job is to create leaders on a multidimensional level. At this point in the game, your primary focus is meeting your team members' personal development needs. Of course, this will not be an instant shift, but you can start developing your leadership tribe now. I am going to give you a few suggestions, however you can also pull from ideas, tools and resources that you used to become the incredible leader that you are today.

The first suggestion is networking. I used to hate networking, and to be frank on many levels I still do. I do not like to label myself, but I would say, I have the tendencies of an introvert, so networking takes a lot of energy from me. Just a little side note, as we are speaking about introverts. When you are developing leaders do not ignore the "introverts." They make some of the best leaders, because they would prefer to be in the background and let their teams shine first. The difference between introverts and extroverts is the way that they release and recharge their energy. Introverts tend to do their best work in private where they can focus and think. It takes a lot of energy for introverts to be in the limelight and in the presence of others constantly. They need to retreat to solitude to recharge. Extroverts are the opposite. They do their best work in groups; they get charged up when they are amongst people and in the limelight. It takes a lot of energy from an extrovert to be alone and in solitude.

Needless to say that although I was uncomfortable in networking situations, I quickly realized that networking is truly important. It allowed me to make valuable connections with individuals that were outside of my immediate circle. By encouraging networking, you will allow your tribe to develop authentic connections for when you are no longer there to toot their horn for them. They will be able to toot their own horns and ask for what they want or need. The way that you could provide your tribe with networking opportunities within the organization is to have members attend interdepartmental meetings and work on cross-functional teams. Networking allows your tribe to branch out beyond their immediate co-workers who they already know, so that when your tribe member enters into their own leadership role, they would already have some of their connections established.

As a leader, you do a lot of public speaking. Find ways for members of your tribe to gain that experience, if you feel that public speaking is necessary for them just as it is for you given that you do a lot of it in your current role. Have your team member do the speaking instead of you so they can get that experience. Have them take turns presenting different topics that are relevant to the team, anything to get them comfortable speaking in front of a group of people, including strangers. Suggesting or providing opportunities for them to join Toastmasters is a great option as well.

You may provide them with opportunities to take the lead of some projects so that they can develop their project management skills. By being the lead of the project, they are responsible for delegating and ensuring that those involved get their tasks completed on time and on budget. If they struggle a little that is okay, this will allow them to develop their problem-solving skills, let them figure out what they need to succeed. Introduce them to resources that you may feel will help them with the solution. They will gain understanding of what it takes to successfully implement a project and to do what you do well.

Be a mentor to them, give them books to read on leadership and meet with them over lunch to discuss it. This will help them formulate what kind of leader they should be, and they can discuss it with you so they can figure out how to start testing it out. Meet with your employees one-on-one to discuss their goals, the ideas they want to implement or any struggles they are facing and want to share. Create an environment where the mentality of ownership can grow within your tribe. It's easy to teach your team about leadership concepts, but what they need is to feel that they are trusted, valued and an impactful part of the organization. Trust them, give them the authority to make decisions, listen to them and implement their ideas because when they feel they are part of your company or your team they will rise to the occasion and want to follow your lead and emerge as leaders themselves. As mentioned before, your tribe is a reflection of you.

Align yourself with your true essence, so that you can connect and unite your purpose and transform yourself into the leader that you are which allows you to empower and inspire others to live a life of excellence.

ACTION STEPS TO TAKE NOW

- Go through your team list, identify what you see as each employee's strength. Discuss this with them. Learn from them what their professional goals are and brainstorm on a plan with them to facilitate them reaching their goals.

This world is screaming for better leaders in our communities, businesses, organizations and in our homes. It is so exciting that you have an opportunity to play a part in developing other intentional, impactful leaders. With them, imagine the world we would have. We would have a world filled with love.